# CSS Text

*Eric A. Meyer*

O'REILLY®

Beijing · Cambridge · Farnham · Köln · Sebastopol · Tokyo

## CSS Text

by Eric A. Meyer

Printed in the United States of America.

Published by O'Reilly Media, Inc., 1005 Gravenstein Highway North, Sebastopol, CA 95472.

O'Reilly books may be purchased for educational, business, or sales promotional use. Online editions are also available for most titles (*http://my.safaribooksonline.com*). For more information, contact our corporate/institutional sales department: 800-998-9938 or *corporate@oreilly.com*.

| | |
|---|---|
| **Editors:** Simon St. Laurent and Meghan Blanchette | **Cover Designer:** Karen Montgomery |
| **Production Editor:** Kara Ebrahim | **Interior Designer:** David Futato |
| **Proofreader:** Nicole Shelby | **Illustrator:** Rebecca Demarest |

August 2013:     First Edition

**Revision History for the First Edition:**

2013-08-21:   First release

See *http://oreilly.com/catalog/errata.csp?isbn=9781449373740* for release details.

ISBN: 978-1-449-37374-0

[LSI]

# Table of Contents

# Preface

## Conventions Used in This Book

The following typographical conventions are used in this book:

*Italic*

Indicates new terms, URLs, email addresses, filenames, and file extensions.

`Constant width`

Used for program listings, as well as within paragraphs to refer to program elements such as variable or function names, databases, data types, environment variables, statements, and keywords.

**`Constant width bold`**

Shows commands or other text that should be typed literally by the user.

*`Constant width italic`*

Shows text that should be replaced with user-supplied values or by values determined by context.

 This icon signifies a tip, suggestion, or general note.

 This icon indicates a warning or caution.

# Safari® Books Online

 Safari Books Online (*www.safaribooksonline.com*) is an on-demand digital library that delivers expert content in both book and video form from the world's leading authors in technology and business.

Technology professionals, software developers, web designers, and business and creative professionals use Safari Books Online as their primary resource for research, problem solving, learning, and certification training.

Safari Books Online offers a range of product mixes and pricing programs for organizations, government agencies, and individuals. Subscribers have access to thousands of books, training videos, and prepublication manuscripts in one fully searchable database from publishers like O'Reilly Media, Prentice Hall Professional, Addison-Wesley Professional, Microsoft Press, Sams, Que, Peachpit Press, Focal Press, Cisco Press, John Wiley & Sons, Syngress, Morgan Kaufmann, IBM Redbooks, Packt, Adobe Press, FT Press, Apress, Manning, New Riders, McGraw-Hill, Jones & Bartlett, Course Technology, and dozens more. For more information about Safari Books Online, please visit us online.

# How to Contact Us

Please address comments and questions concerning this book to the publisher:

O'Reilly Media, Inc.
1005 Gravenstein Highway North
Sebastopol, CA 95472
800-998-9938 (in the United States or Canada)
707-829-0515 (international or local)
707-829-0104 (fax)

We have a web page for this book, where we list errata, examples, and any additional information. You can access this page at *http://oreil.ly/csstext-meyer*.

To comment or ask technical questions about this book, send email to *bookquestions@oreilly.com*.

For more information about our books, courses, conferences, and news, see our website at *http://www.oreilly.com*.

Find us on Facebook: *http://facebook.com/oreilly*

Follow us on Twitter: *http://twitter.com/oreillymedia*

Watch us on YouTube: *http://www.youtube.com/oreillymedia*

# Text Properties

Sure, a lot of web design involves picking the right colors and getting the coolest look for your pages, but when it comes right down to it, you probably spend more of your time worrying about where text will go and how it will look. Such concerns gave rise to HTML tags such as <FONT> and <CENTER>, which allow you some measure of control over the appearance and placement of text.

Because text is so important, there are many CSS properties that affect it in one way or another. What is the difference between text and fonts? Simply, text is the content, and fonts are used to display that content. Using text properties, you can affect the position of text in relation to the rest of the line, superscript it, underline it, and change the capitalization. You can even simulate, to a limited degree, the use of a typewriter's Tab key.

## Indentation and Horizontal Alignment

Let's start with a discussion of how you can affect the horizontal positioning of text within a line. Think of these basic actions as the same types of steps you might take to create a newsletter or write a report.

### Indenting Text

Indenting the first line of a paragraph on a web page is one of the most sought-after text-formatting effects. (Eliminating the blank line between paragraphs is a close second.) Some sites used to create the illusion of indented text by placing a small transparent image before the first letter in a paragraph, which shoves the text over. Thanks to CSS, there's a much better way to indent text, called `text-indent`.

# text-indent

*Values:*
    *<length>* | *<percentage>* | `inherit`

*Initial value:*
    `0`

*Applies to:*
    Block-level elements

*Inherited:*
    Yes

*Percentages:*
    Refer to the width of the containing block

*Computed value:*
    For percentage values, as specified; for length values, the absolute length

Using `text-indent`, the first line of any element can be indented by a given length—even if that length is negative. The most common use for this property is, of course, to indent the first line of a paragraph:

```
p {text-indent: 3em;}
```

This rule will cause the first line of any paragraph to be indented three ems, as shown in Figure 1.

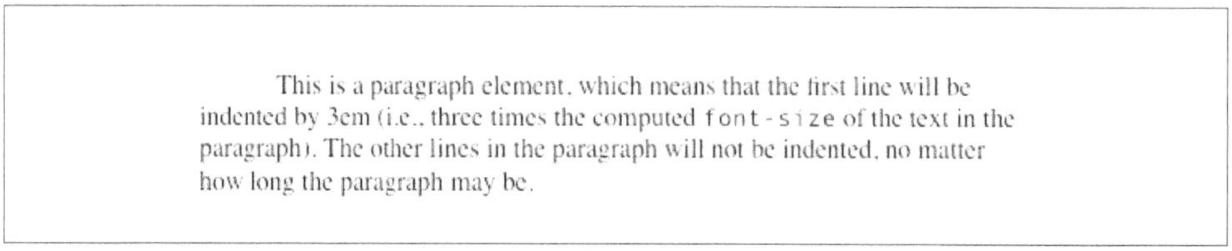

This is a paragraph element, which means that the first line will be indented by 3em (i.e., three times the computed font-size of the text in the paragraph). The other lines in the paragraph will not be indented, no matter how long the paragraph may be.

*Figure 1. Text indenting*

In general, you can apply `text-indent` to any block-level element. You can't apply it to inline elements or on replaced elements such as images. However, if you have an image within the first line of a block-level element, like a paragraph, it will be shifted over with the rest of the text in the line.

If you want to "indent" the first line of an inline element, you can create the effect with left padding or margin.

You can also set negative values for text-indent, a technique that leads to a number of interesting effects. The most common use is a "hanging indent," where the first line hangs out to the left of the rest of the element:

```
p {text-indent: -4em;}
```

Be careful when setting a negative value for text-indent; the first three words ("This is a") may be chopped off by the left edge of the browser window. To avoid display problems, I recommend you use a margin or some padding to accommodate the negative indentation:

```
p {text-indent: -4em; padding-left: 4em;}
```

Negative indents can, however, be used to your advantage. Consider the following example, demonstrated in Figure 2, which adds a floated image to the mix:

```
p.hang {text-indent: -25px;}

<img src="star.gif" style="width: 60px; height: 60px;
float: left;" alt="An image of a five-pointed star."/>
<p class="hang"> This paragraph has a negatively indented first
line, which overlaps the floated image that precedes the text.  Subsequent
lines do not overlap the image, since they are not indented in any way.</p>
```

> This paragraph has a negatively indented first line, which overlaps the floated image that precedes the text. Subsequent lines do not overlap the image, since they are not indented in any way.

*Figure 2. A floated image and negative text indenting*

A variety of interesting designs can be achieved using this simple technique.

Any unit of length, including percentage values, may be used with text-indent. In the following case, the percentage refers to the width of the parent element of the element being indented. In other words, if you set the indent value to 10%, the first line of an affected element will be indented by 10 percent of its parent element's width, as shown in Figure 3:

```
div {width: 400px;}
p {text-indent: 10%;}

<div>
<p>This paragraph is contained inside a DIV, which is 400px wide, so the
first line of the paragraph is indented 40px (400 * 10% = 40).  This is
```

```
because percentages are computed with respect to the width of the element.</p>
</div>
```

> This paragraph is contained inside a DIV, which is
> 400px wide, so the first line of the paragraph is indented 40px
> (400 * 10% = 40). This is because percentages are computed
> with respect to the width of the element.

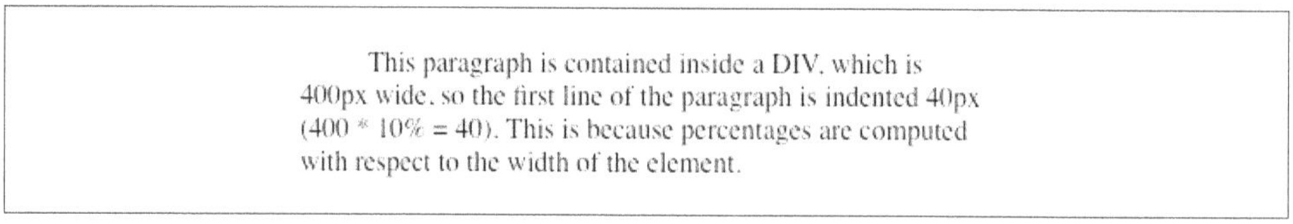

*Figure 3. Text indenting with percentages*

Note that this indentation only applies to the first line of an element, even if you insert line breaks. The interesting part about `text-indent` is that because it's inherited, it can have unexpected effects. For example, consider the following markup, which is illustrated in Figure 4:

```
div#outer {width: 500px;}
div#inner {text-indent: 10%;}
p {width: 200px;}

<div id="outer">
<div id="inner">
This first line of the DIV is indented by 50 pixels.
<p>
This paragraph is 200px wide, and the first line of the paragraph
is indented 50px.  This is because computed values for 'text-indent'
are inherited, instead of the declared values.
</p>
</div>
</div>
```

> This first line of the DIV is indented by 50 pixels.
>
> This paragraph is
> 200px wide, and the first line
> of the paragraph is indented
> 50px. This is because
> computed values for
> text-indent are inherited,
> instead of the declared values.

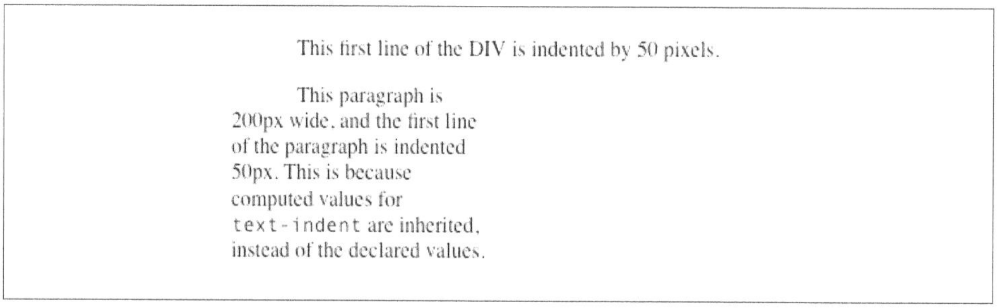

*Figure 4. Inherited text indenting*

## Horizontal Alignment

Even more basic than `text-indent` is the property `text-align`, which affects how the lines of text in an element are aligned with respect to one another.

# text-align

*CSS 2.1 values:*
    left | center | right | justify | inherit

*CSS3 values:*
    [ [ start | end | left | right | center ] || <*string*> ] | justify | match-parent |
    start end | inherit

*Initial value:*
    In CSS3, start; in CSS 2.1, user agent-specific, likely depending on writing
    direction

*Applies to:*
    Block-level elements

*Inherited:*
    Yes

*Computed value:*
    As specified, except in the case of match-parent

*Note:*
    CSS2 included a <*string*> value that was dropped from CSS 2.1 due to a lack of
    implementation

The quickest way to understand how these values work is to examine Figure 5, which
sticks with three of the CSS 2.1 values for the moment.

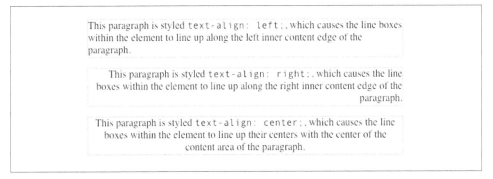

*Figure 5. Selected behaviors of the text-align property*

Obviously, the values left, right, and center cause the text within elements to be
aligned exactly as described. Because text-align applies only to block-level elements,

such as paragraphs, there's no way to center an anchor within its line without aligning the rest of the line (nor would you want to, since that would likely cause text overlap).

Historically, which is to say under CSS 2.1 rules, the default value of text-align is left in left-to-right languages, and right in right-to-left languages. (CSS 2.1 had no notion of vertical writing modes.) In CSS3, left and right are mapped to the start or end edge, respectively, of a vertical language. This is illustrated in Figure 6.

As you no doubt expect, center causes each line of text to be centered within the element. Although you may be tempted to believe that text-align: center is the same as the <CENTER> element, it's actually quite different. <CENTER> affected not only text, but also centered whole elements, such as tables. text-align does not control the alignment of elements, only their inline content. Figures 5 and 6 illustrate this clearly in various writing directions.

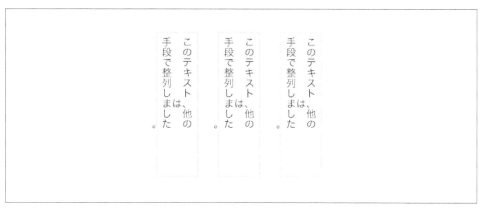

*Figure 6. Left, right, and center in vertical writing modes*

### Start and end alignment

CSS3 (which is to say, the "CSS Text Module Level 3" specification) added a number of new values to text-align, and even changed the default property value as compared to CSS 2.1.

The new default value of start means that the text is aligned to the start edge of its line box. In left-to-right languages like English, that's the left edge; in right-to-left languages such as Hebrew, it's the right edge. In vertical languages, for that matter, it will be the top or bottom, depending on the writing direction. The upshot is that the default value is much more aware of the document's language direction while leaving the default behavior the same in the vast majority of existing cases.

In a like manner, end aligns text with the end edge of each line box—the right edge in LTR languages, the left edge in RTL languages, and so forth. The effects of these values are shown in Figure 7.

*Figure 7. Start and end alignment*

And then there's the value `start end`, which is declared like so:

```
p {text-align: start end;}
```

This is a fascinating, and so far unsupported, value of `text-align`. The effect is that the first line of the element, as well as any line that immediately follows a line break, uses `start` alignment. The rest of the lines in the element use `end` alignment. (It may be dropped from the CSS3 module if nobody starts supporting it.)

### Justified text

An often-overlooked alignment property is `justify`, which raises some issues of its own. In justified text, both ends of a line of text are placed at the inner edge of the parent element, as Figure 8 shows. Then, the spacing between words and letters is adjusted so that each line is precisely the same length. Justified text is common in the print world (for example, in this book), but under CSS, a few extra considerations come into play.

This paragraph is styled text-align: justify;, which causes the line boxes within the element to align their left and right edges to the left and right inner content edges of the paragraph. The exception is the last line box, whose right edge does not align with the right content edge of the paragraph. (In right-to-left languages, the left edge of the last line box would not be so aligned.)

This paragraph is styled text-align: justify;, which causes the line boxes within the element to align their left and right edges to the left and right inner content edges of the paragraph. The exception is the last line box, whose right edge does not align with the right content edge of the paragraph. (In right-to-left languages, the left edge of the last line box would not be so aligned.)

*Figure 8. Justified text*

The user agent—and not CSS, at least as of mid-2013—determines how justified text should be stretched to fill the space between the left and right edges of the parent. Some browsers, for example, might add extra space only between words, while others might distribute the extra space between letters (although the CSS specification states that "user agents may not further increase or decrease the inter-character space" if the property `letter-spacing` has been assigned a length value). Other user agents may reduce space on some lines, thus mashing the text together a bit more than usual. All of these possibilities will affect the appearance of an element, and may even change its height, depending on how many lines of text result from the user agent's justification choices.

## String alignment

String alignment is an interesting case, one that has been lurking throughout the history of CSS without actually gaining traction. The easiest way to explain it is to show some code and the results (Figure 9):

```
table[summary="Daily Sales"] th {text-align: "/";}
table[summary="Daily Sales"] td {text-align: ".";}

<table summary="Daily Sales">
<tr><th>Mon 4/8</th><td>$12,122.13</td></tr>
<tr><th>Tue 4/9</th><td>$13,729.10</td></tr>
<tr><th>Wed 4/10</th><td>$9,447</td></tr>
<tr><th>Thu 4/11</th><td>$10,308.76</td></tr>
<tr><th>Fri 4/12</th><td>$999.99</td></tr>
</table>
```

| | |
|---|---|
| Mon 4/8 | $12,122.13 |
| Tue 4/9 | $13,729.10 |
| Wed 4/10 | $9,447 |
| Thu 4/11 | $10,308.76 |
| Fri 4/12 | $999.99 |

*Figure 9. String alignment*

As Figure 9 shows, all the cells' contents are aligned such that the "." characters line up along a vertical line (since this is a horizontal language). Had the CSS actually been text-align: "," then the cells would all have lined up on the commas.

The problem, as always, is that string alignment still isn't supported by browsers, and may be once again dropped from the specification. (Figure 9 was faked, I'm sorry to say.)

## Parent matching

There's one more value to be covered, which is match-parent. This isn't supported by browsers, but its intent is mostly covered by inherit anyway. The idea is, if you declare text-align: match-parent, the alignment of the element will match the alignment of its parent. So far, that sounds exactly like inherit, but there's a difference: if the parent's alignment value is start or end, the result of match-parent is to assign a computed value of left or right to the element. That wouldn't happen with inherit, which would simply apply start or end to the element with no changes.

## Aligning the Last Line

There may be times when you want to align the text in the very last line of an element differently than you did the rest of the content. For example, you might left-align the last line of an otherwise fully justified block of text, or choose to swap from left to center alignment. For those situations, there is `text-align-last`.

---

### text-align-last

*Values:*
    auto | start | end | left | right | center | justify

*Initial value:*
    auto

*Applies to:*
    Block-level elements

*Inherited:*
    Yes

*Computed value:*
    As specified

---

As with `text-align`, the quickest way to understand how these values work is to examine Figure 10.

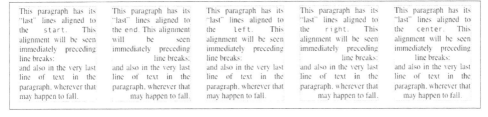

*Figure 10. Differently aligned last lines*

As you can see, the last lines of the elements are aligned independently of the rest of the elements, according to the elements' `text-align-last` values.

A close study of Figure 10 will reveal that there's more at play than just the last lines of block-level elements. In fact, `text-align-last` applies to any line of text that immediately precedes a forced line break, whether or not said line break is triggered by the end of an element. Thus, a line break occasioned by a `<br>` tag will make the line of text immediately before that break use the value of `text-align-last`. So too will the last line of text in a block-level element, since a line break is generated by the element's closure.

There are two more interesting wrinkles in `text-align-last`. The first is that if the first line of text in an element is also the last line of text in the element, then the value of `text-align-last` takes precedence over the value of `text-align`. Thus, the following styles will result in a centered paragraph, not a start-aligned paragraph:

```
p {text-align: start; text-align-last: center;}

<p>A paragraph.</p>
```

The second, closely related, wrinkle is that `text-align-last` is ignored if the element's `text-align` value is `start end`. In other words, in the following case, the text will *not* be centered:

```
p {text-align: START end; text-align-last: center;}

<p>A paragraph.</p>
```

 As of mid-2013, support for `text-align-last` was limited to a prefixed Gecko property, `-moz-text-align-last`.

# Vertical Alignment

Now that we've covered horizontal alignment, let's move on to vertical alignment. Since the construction of lines is a very complex topic that merits its own small book, I'll just stick to a quick overview here.

## The Height of Lines

The `line-height` property refers to the distance between the baselines of lines of text rather than the size of the font, and it determines the amount by which the height of each element's box is increased or decreased. In the most basic cases, specifying `line-height` is a way to increase (or decrease) the vertical space between lines of text, but this is a misleadingly simple way of looking at how `line-height` works. `line-height` controls the *leading*, which is the extra space between lines of text above and beyond the font's size. In other words, the difference between the value of `line-height` and the size of the font is the leading.

# line-height

*Values:*
   *<length>* | *<percentage>* | *<number>* | normal | inherit

*Initial value:*
   normal

*Applies to:*
   All elements (but see text regarding replaced and block-level elements)

*Inherited:*
   Yes

*Percentages:*
   Relative to the font size of the element

*Computed value:*
   For length and percentage values, the absolute value; otherwise, as specified

When applied to a block-level element, line-height defines the minimum distance between text baselines within that element. Note that it defines a minimum, not an absolute value, and baselines of text can wind up being pushed further apart than the value of line-height. line-height does not affect layout for replaced elements, but it still applies to them.

## Constructing a line

Every element in a line of text generates a *content area*, which is determined by the size of the font. This content area in turn generates an *inline box* that is, in the absence of any other factors, exactly equal to the content area. The leading generated by line-height is one of the factors that increases or decreases the height of each inline box.

To determine the leading for a given element, simply subtract the computed value of font-size from the computed value of line-height. That value is the total amount of leading. And remember, it can be a negative number. The leading is then divided in half, and each half-leading is applied to the top and bottom of the content area. The result is the inline box for that element.

As an example, let's say the font-size (and therefore the content area) is 14 pixels tall, and the line-height is computed to 18 pixels. The difference (4 pixels) is divided in half, and each half is applied to the top and bottom of the content area. This creates an inline box that is 18 pixels tall, with 2 extra pixels above and below the content area. This sounds like a roundabout way to describe how line-height works, but there are excellent reasons for the description.

Once all of the inline boxes have been generated for a given line of content, they are then considered in the construction of the line box. A line box is exactly as tall as needed to enclose the top of the tallest inline box and the bottom of the lowest inline box. Figure 11 shows a diagram of this process.

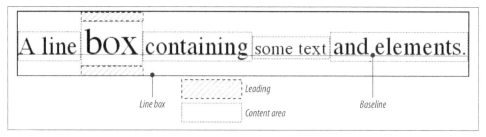

*Figure 11. Line box diagram*

### Assigning values to line-height

Let's now consider the possible values of line-height. If you use the default value of normal, the user agent must calculate the vertical space between lines. Values can vary by user agent, but they're generally 1.2 times the size of the font, which makes line boxes taller than the value of font-size for a given element.

Most values are simple length measures (e.g., 18px or 2em). Be aware that even if you use a valid length measurement, such as 4cm, the browser (or the operating system) may be using an incorrect metric for real-world measurements, so the line height may not show up as exactly four centimeters on your monitor.

em, ex, and percentage values are calculated with respect to the font-size of the element. The markup is relatively straightforward, and the results are shown in Figure 12:

```
body {line-height: 18px; font-size: 16px;}
p.cl1 {line-height: 1.5em;}
p.cl2 {font-size: 10px; line-height: 150%;}
p.cl3 {line-height: 0.33in;}

<p>This paragraph inherits a 'line-height' of 14px from the body, as well as
a 'font-size' of 13px.</p>
<p class="cl1">This paragraph has a 'line-height' of 27px(18 * 1.5), so
it will have slightly more line-height than usual.</p>
<p class="cl2">This paragraph has a 'line-height' of 15px (10 * 150%), so
it will have slightly more line-height than usual.</p>
<p class="cl3">This paragraph has a 'line-height' of 0.33in, so it will have
slightly more line-height than usual.</p>
```

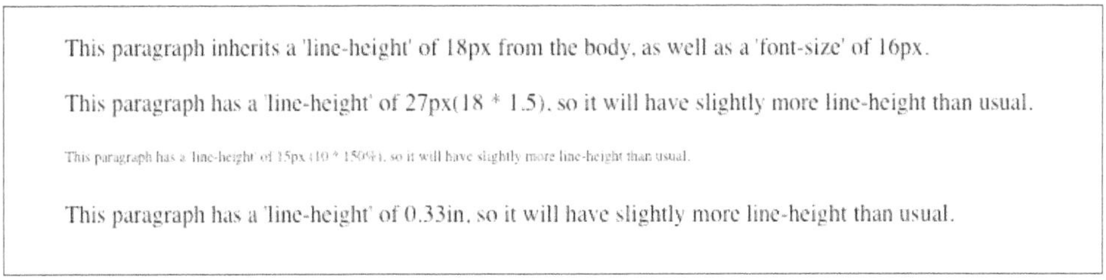

This paragraph inherits a 'line-height' of 18px from the body, as well as a 'font-size' of 16px.

This paragraph has a 'line-height' of 27px(18 * 1.5), so it will have slightly more line-height than usual.

This paragraph has a 'line-height' of 15px (10 * 150%), so it will have slightly more line-height than usual.

This paragraph has a 'line-height' of 0.33in, so it will have slightly more line-height than usual.

*Figure 12. Simple calculations with the line-height property*

## Line-height and inheritance

When the line-height is inherited by one block-level element from another, things get a bit trickier. line-height values inherit from the parent element as computed from the parent, not the child. The results of the following markup are shown in Figure 13. It probably wasn't what the author had in mind:

```
body {font-size: 10px;}
div {line-height: 1em;}  /* computes to '10px' */
p {font-size: 18px;}

<div>
<p>This paragraph's 'font-size' is 18px, but the inherited 'line-height'
value is only 10px.  This may cause the lines of text to overlap each
other by a small amount.</p>
</div>
```

This paragraph's 'font-size' is 18px, but the inherited 'line-height' value is only 10px. This may cause the lines of text to overlap each other by a small amount.

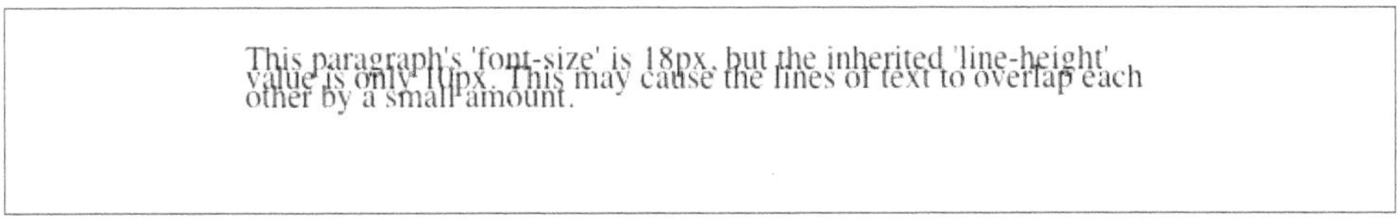

*Figure 13. Small line-height, large font-size, slight problem*

Why are the lines so close together? Because the computed line-height value of 10px was inherited by the paragraph from its parent div. One solution to the small line-height problem depicted in Figure 13 is to set an explicit line-height for every element, but that's not very practical. A better alternative is to specify a number, which actually sets a scaling factor:

```
body {font-size: 10px;}
div {line-height: 1;}
p {font-size: 18px;}
```

When you specify a number, you cause the scaling factor to be an inherited value instead of a computed value. The number will be applied to the element and all of its child elements, so that each element has a line-height calculated with respect to its own font-size (see Figure 14):

```
div {line-height: 1.5;}
p {font-size: 18px;}

<div>
<p>This paragraph's 'font-size' is 18px, and since the 'line-height'
set for the parent div is 1.5, the 'line-height' for this paragraph
is 27px (18 * 1.5).</p>
</div>
```

This paragraph's 'font-size' is 18px, and since the 'line-height' set for
the parent div is 1.5, the 'line-height' for this paragraph is 27px (18 *
1.5).

*Figure 14. Using line-height factors to overcome inheritance problems*

Though it seems like line-height distributes extra space both above and below each line of text, it actually adds (or subtracts) a certain amount from the top and bottom of an inline element's content area to create an inline box. Assume that the default font-size of a paragraph is 12pt and consider the following:

```
p {line-height: 16pt;}
```

Since the "inherent" line height of 12-point text is 12 points, the preceding rule will place an extra 4 points of space around each line of text in the paragraph. This extra amount is divided in two, with half going above each line and the other half below. You now have 16 points between the baselines, which is an indirect result of how the extra space is apportioned.

If you specify the value inherit, then the element will use the computed value for its parent element. This isn't really any different than allowing the value to inherit naturally, except in terms of specificity and cascade resolution.

Now that you have a basic grasp of how lines are constructed, let's talk about vertically aligning elements relative to the line box.

## Vertically Aligning Text

If you've ever used the elements sup and sub (the superscript and subscript elements), or used an image with markup such as <img src="foo.gif" align="middle">, then you've done some rudimentary vertical alignment. In CSS, the vertical-align property applies only to inline elements and replaced elements such as images and form inputs. vertical-align is not an inherited property.

# vertical-align

*Values:*
    baseline | sub | super | top | text-top | middle | bottom | text-bottom |
    <percentage> | <length> | inherit

*Initial value:*
    baseline

*Applies to:*
    Inline elements and table cells

*Inherited:*
    No

*Percentages:*
    Refer to the value of line-height for the element

*Computed value:*
    For percentage and length values, the absolute length; otherwise, as specified

*Note:*
    When applied to table cells, only the values baseline, top, middle, and bottom are
    recognized

vertical-align accepts any one of eight keywords, a percentage value, or a length value. The keywords are a mix of the familiar and unfamiliar: baseline (the default value), sub, super, bottom, text-bottom, middle, top, and text-top. We'll examine how each keyword works in relation to inline elements.

Remember: vertical-align does *not* affect the alignment of content within a block-level element. You can, however, use it to affect the vertical alignment of elements within table cells.

## Baseline alignment

vertical-align: baseline forces the baseline of an element to align with the baseline of its parent. Browsers, for the most part, do this anyway, since you'd obviously expect the bottoms of all text elements in a line to be aligned.

If a vertically aligned element doesn't have a baseline—that is, if it's an image, a form input, or another replaced element—then the bottom of the element is aligned with the baseline of its parent, as Figure 15 shows:

```
img {vertical-align: baseline;}

<p>The image found in this paragraph <img src="dot.gif" alt="A dot" /> has its
bottom edge aligned with the baseline of the text in the paragraph.</p>
```

> The image found in this paragraph ● has its bottom edge aligned with the
> baseline of the text in the paragraph.

*Figure 15. Baseline alignment of an image*

This alignment rule is important because it causes some web browsers to always put a replaced element's bottom edge on the baseline, even if there is no other text in the line. For example, let's say you have an image in a table cell all by itself. The image may actually be on a baseline, but in some browsers, the space below the baseline causes a gap to appear beneath the image. Other browsers will "shrink-wrap" the image with the table cell, and no gap will appear. The gap behavior is correct, according to the CSS Working Group, despite its lack of appeal to most authors.

 See the aged and yet still relevant article "Images, Tables, and Mysterious Gaps" (*http://mzl.la/19E2dJ7*) for a more detailed explanation of gap behavior and ways to work around it.

### Superscripting and subscripting

The declaration `vertical-align: sub` causes an element to be subscripted, meaning that its baseline (or bottom, if it's a replaced element) is lowered with respect to its parent's baseline. The specification doesn't define the distance the element is lowered, so it may vary depending on the user agent.

`super` is the opposite of `sub`; it raises the element's baseline (or bottom of a replaced element) with respect to the parent's baseline. Again, the distance the text is raised depends on the user agent.

Note that the values `sub` and `super` do *not* change the element's font size, so subscripted or superscripted text will not become smaller (or larger). Instead, any text in the sub- or superscripted element should be, by default, the same size as text in the parent element, as illustrated by Figure 16:

```
span.raise {vertical-align: super;}
span.lower {vertical-align: sub;}

<p>This paragraph contains <span class="raise">superscripted</span>
and <span class="lower">subscripted</span> text.</P>
```

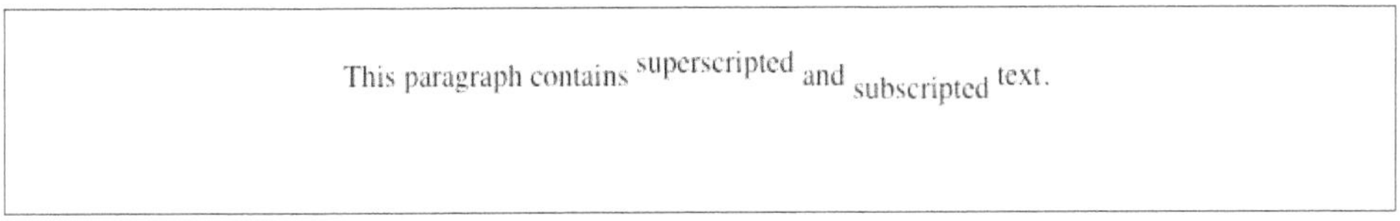

This paragraph contains <sup>superscripted</sup> and <sub>subscripted</sub> text.

*Figure 16. Superscript and subscript alignment*

 If you wish to make super- or subscripted text smaller than the text of its parent element, you can do so using the property font-size.

## Bottom feeding

vertical-align: bottom aligns the bottom of the element's inline box with the bottom of the line box. For example, the following markup results in Figure 17:

```
.feeder {vertical-align: bottom;}

<p>This paragraph, as you can see quite clearly, contains
a <img src="tall.gif" alt="tall" class="feeder" /> image and
a <img src="short.gif" alt="short" class="feeder" /> image,
and then some text that is not tall.</p>
```

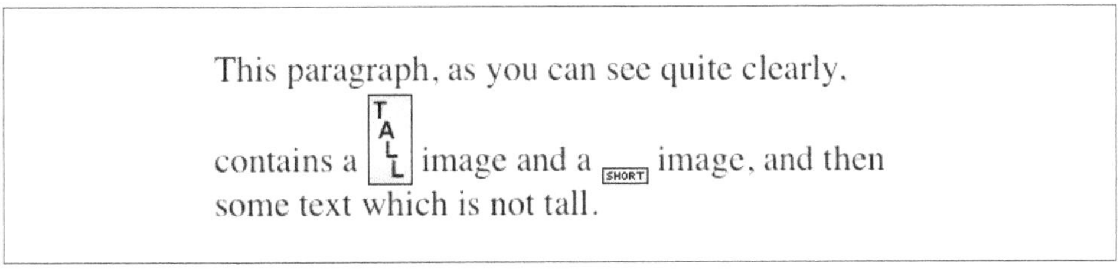

This paragraph, as you can see quite clearly, contains a [TALL] image and a [SHORT] image, and then some text which is not tall.

*Figure 17. Bottom alignment*

The second line of the paragraph in Figure 17 contains two inline elements, whose bottom edges are aligned with each other. They're also below the baseline of the text.

vertical-align: text-bottom refers to the bottom of the text in the line. For the purposes of this value, replaced elements, or any other kinds of non-text elements, are ignored. Instead, a "default" text box is considered. This default box is derived from the font-size of the parent element. The bottom of the aligned element's inline box is then aligned with the bottom of the default text box. Thus, given the following markup, you get a result like the one shown in Figure 18:

```
img.tbot {vertical-align: text-bottom;}

<p>Here: a <img src="tall.gif" style="vertical-align: middle;" alt="tall" />
image, and then a <img src="short.gif" class="tbot" alt="short" /> image.</p>
```

*Figure 18. Text-bottom alignment*

## Getting on top

Employing vertical-align: top has the opposite effect of bottom. Likewise, vertical-align: text-top is the reverse of text-bottom. Figure 19 shows how the following markup would be rendered:

```
.up {vertical-align: top;}
.textup {vertical-align: text-top;}

<p>Here: a <img src="tall.gif" alt="tall image"> tall image, and then
<span class="up">some text</span> that's been vertically aligned.</p>
<p>Here: a <img src="tall.gif" class="textup" alt="tall"> image that's been
vertically    aligned,    and    then    a    <img    src="short.gif"    class="textup"
alt="short" />
image that's similarly aligned.</p>
```

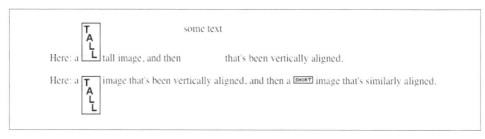

*Figure 19. Aligning with the top and text-top of a line*

Of course, the exact position of this alignment will depend on which elements are in the line, how tall they are, and the size of the parent element's font.

## In the middle

There's the value middle, which is usually (but not always) applied to images. It does not have the exact effect you might assume given its name. middle aligns the middle of an inline element's box with a point that is 0.5ex above the baseline of the parent element, where 1ex is defined relative to the font-size for the parent element. Figure 20 shows this in more detail.

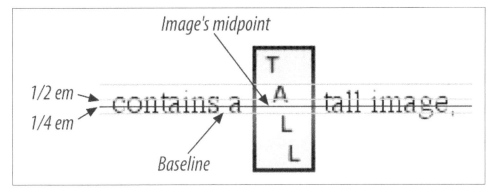

*Figure 20. Precise detail of middle alignment*

Since most user agents treat 1ex as one-half em, middle usually aligns the vertical mid-point of an element with a point one-quarter em above the parent's baseline, though this is not a defined distance and so can vary from one user agent to another.

## Percentages

Percentages don't let you simulate align="middle" for images. Instead, setting a percentage value for vertical-align raises or lowers the baseline of the element (or the bottom edge of a replaced element) by the amount declared, with respect to the parent's baseline. (The percentage you specify is calculated as a percentage of line-height for the element, *not* its parent.) Positive percentage values raise the element, and negative values lower it. Depending on how the text is raised or lowered, it can appear to be placed in adjacent lines, as shown in Figure 21, so take care when using percentage values:

```
sub {vertical-align: -100%;}
sup {vertical-align: 100%;}

<p>We can either <sup>soar to new heights</sup> or, instead,
<sub>sink into despair...</sub></p>
```

                        soar to new heights
    We can either                          or , instead,
                                                sink into despair...

*Figure 21. Percentages and fun effects*

Let's consider percentage values in more detail. Assume the following:

```
<div style="font-size: 14px; line-height: 18px;">
I felt that, if nothing else, I deserved a
<span style="vertical-align: 50%;">raise</span> for my efforts.
</div>
```

The 50%-aligned span element has its baseline raised nine pixels, which is half of the element's inherited line-height value of 18px, *not* seven pixels.

### Length alignment

Finally, let's consider vertical alignment with a specific length. vertical-align is very straightforward: it shifts an element up or down by the declared distance. Thus, vertical-align: 5px; will shift an element upward five pixels from its unaligned placement. Negative length values shift the element downward. This simple form of alignment did not exist in CSS1, but it was added in CSS2.

It's important to realize that vertically aligned text does not become part of another line, nor does it overlap text in other lines. Consider Figure 22, in which some vertically aligned text appears in the middle of a paragraph.

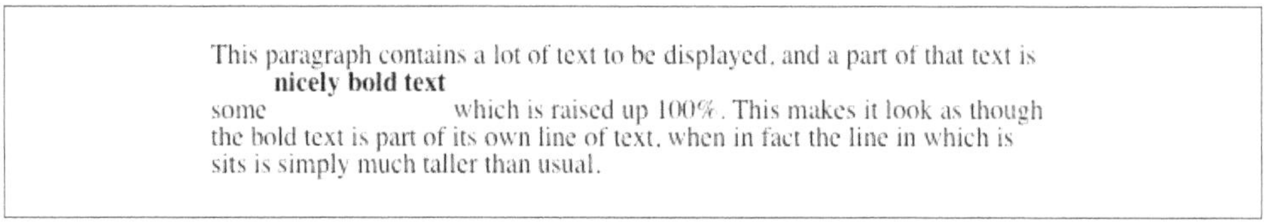

*Figure 22. Vertical alignments can cause lines to get taller*

As you can see, any vertically aligned element can affect the height of the line. Recall the description of a line box, which is exactly as tall as necessary to enclose the top of the tallest inline box and the bottom of the lowest inline box. This includes inline boxes that have been shifted up or down by vertical alignment.

# Word Spacing and Letter Spacing

Now that we've dealt with alignment, let's look at manipulating word and letter spacing. As usual, these properties have some nonintuitive issues.

## Word Spacing

The word-spacing property accepts a positive or negative length. This length is *added* to the standard space between words. In effect, word-spacing is used to *modify* inter-word spacing. Therefore, the default value of normal is the same as setting a value of zero (0).

# word-spacing

*Values:*
　　<*length*> | normal | inherit

*Initial value:*
　　normal

*Applies to:*
　　All elements

*Inherited:*
　　Yes

*Computed value:*
　　For normal, the absolute length 0; otherwise, the absolute length

If you supply a positive length value, then the space between words will increase. Setting a negative value for word-spacing brings words closer together:

```
p.spread {word-spacing: 0.5em;}
p.tight {word-spacing: -0.5em;}
p.base {word-spacing: normal;}
p.norm {word-spacing: 0;}

<p class="spread">The spaces between words in this paragraph will be increased
    by 0.5em.</p>
<p class="tight">The spaces between words in this paragraph will be decreased
    by 0.5em.</p>
<p class="base">The spaces between words in this paragraph will be normal.</p>
<p class="norm">The spaces between words in this paragraph will be normal.</p>
```

Manipulating these settings has the effect shown in Figure 23.

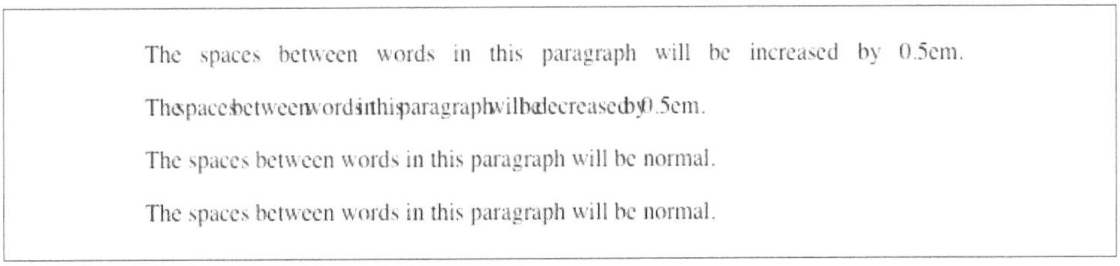

The spaces between words in this paragraph will be increased by 0.5em.

Thespacebetweenwordsinthisparagraphwilbedecreasedby0.5em.

The spaces between words in this paragraph will be normal.

The spaces between words in this paragraph will be normal.

*Figure 23. Changing the space between words*

So far, I haven't actually given you a precise definition of "word." In the simplest CSS terms, a "word" is any string of nonwhitespace characters that is surrounded by whitespace of some kind. This definition has no real semantic meaning; it simply assumes that a document contains words surrounded by one or more whitespace characters. A CSS-aware user agent cannot be expected to decide what is a valid word in a given language and what isn't. This definition, such as it is, means word-spacing is unlikely to work in any languages that employ pictographs, or non-Roman writing styles. The property allows you to create very unreadable documents, as Figure 24 makes clear. Use word-spacing with care.

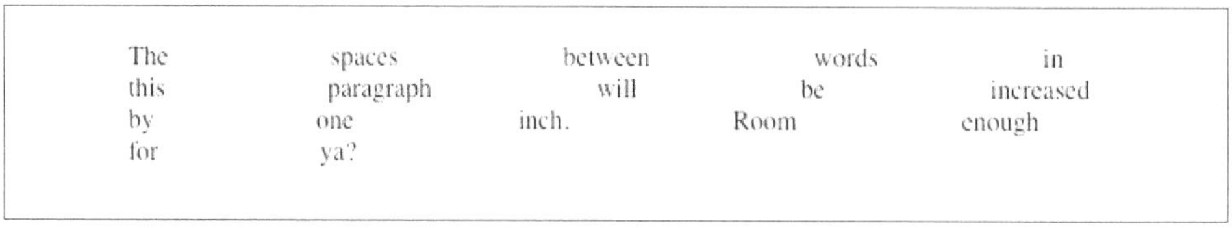

| The | spaces | | between | words | in |
| this | paragraph | | will | be | increased |
| by | one | inch. | | Room | enough |
| for | ya? | | | | |

*Figure 24. Really wide word spacing*

## Letter Spacing

Many of the issues you encounter with word-spacing also occur with letter-spacing. The only real difference between the two is that letter-spacing modifies the space between characters, or letters.

### letter-spacing

*Values:*
    <length> | normal | inherit

*Initial value:*
    normal

*Applies to:*
    All elements

*Inherited:*
    Yes

*Computed value:*
    For length values, the absolute length; otherwise, normal

As with the word-spacing property, the permitted values of letter-spacing include any length. The default keyword is normal (making it the same as letter-spacing: 0). Any length value you enter will increase or decrease the space between letters by that amount. Figure 25 shows the results of the following markup:

```
p {letter-spacing: 0;}     /* identical to 'normal' */
p.spacious {letter-spacing: 0.25em;}
p.tight {letter-spacing: -0.25em;}
```

```
<p>The letters in this paragraph are spaced as normal.</p>
<p class="spacious">The letters in this paragraph are spread out a bit.</p>
<p class="tight">The letters in this paragraph are a bit smashed together.</p>
```

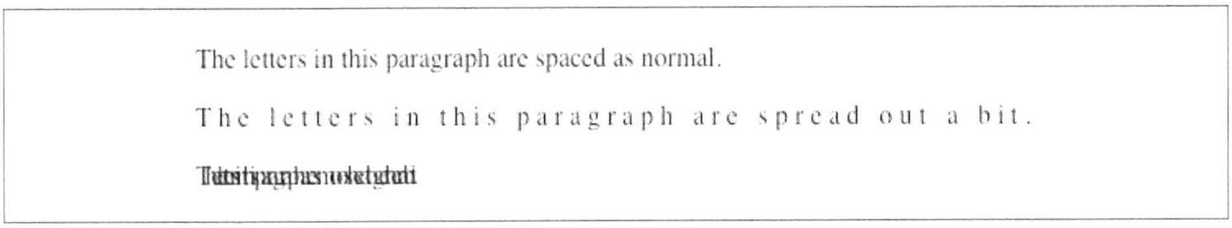

The letters in this paragraph are spaced as normal.

The  letters  in  this  paragraph  are  spread  out  a  bit.

Thistipagnphasuokatgdacti

*Figure 25. Various kinds of letter spacing*

Using letter-spacing to increase emphasis is a time-honored technique. You might
write the following declaration and get an effect like the one shown in Figure 26:

```
strong {letter-spacing: 0.2em;}
```

```
<p>This paragraph contains <strong>strongly emphasized text</strong>
that is spread out for extra emphasis.</p>
```

This paragraph contains **s t r o n g l y  e m p h a s i z e d  t e x t** which is
spread out for extra emphasis.

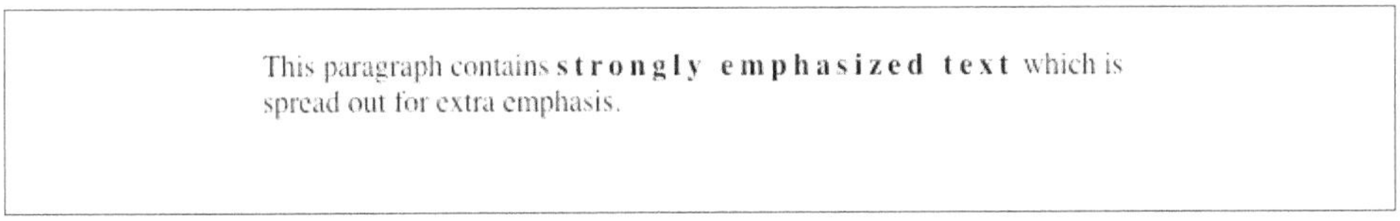

*Figure 26. Using letter-spacing to increase emphasis*

 If a page uses fonts with features like ligatures, and those features are
enabled, then altering letter- or word-spacing can effectively disable
them. Browsers will not re-calculate ligatures or other joins when letter spacing is altered, for example.

## Spacing and Alignment

The value of word-spacing may be influenced by the value of the property text-
align. If an element is justified, the spaces between letters and words may be altered to
fit the text along the full width of the line. This may in turn alter the spacing declared
by the author with word-spacing. If a length value is assigned to letter-spacing, then
it cannot be changed by text-align, but if the value of letter-spacing is normal, then
inter-character spacing may be changed in order to justify the text. CSS does not specify
how the spacing should be calculated, so user agents simply fill it in.

As usual, the child of an element inherits the computed value of that element. You cannot
define a scaling factor for word-spacing or letter-spacing to be inherited in place of

the computed value (as is the case with line-height). As a result, you may run into problems such as those shown in Figure 27:

```
p {letter-spacing: 0.25em; font-size: 20px;}
small {font-size: 50%;}

<p>This spacious paragraph features <small>tiny text that is just
as spacious</small>, even though the author probably wanted the
spacing to be in proportion to the size of the text.</p>
```

This spacious paragraph features tiny text which is just as spacious, even though the author probably wanted the spacing to be in proportion to the size of the text.

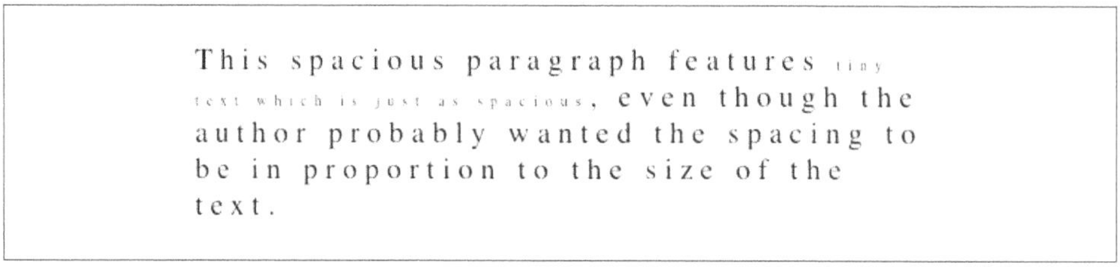

*Figure 27. Inherited letter spacing*

The only way to achieve letter spacing that's in proportion to the size of the text is to set it explicitly, as follows:

```
p {letter-spacing: 0.25em;}
small {font-size: 50%; letter-spacing: 0.25em;}
```

# Text Transformation

Now let's look at ways to manipulate the capitalization of text using the property text-transform.

## text-transform

*Values:*
    uppercase | lowercase | capitalize | none | inherit

*Initial value:*
    none

*Applies to:*
    All elements

*Inherited:*
    Yes

*Computed value:*
    As specified

The default value none leaves the text alone and uses whatever capitalization exists in the source document. As their names imply, uppercase and lowercase convert text into all upper- or lowercase characters. Finally, capitalize capitalizes only the first letter of each word. Figure 28 illustrates each of these settings in a variety of ways:

```
h1 {text-transform: capitalize;}
strong {text-transform: uppercase;}
p.cummings {text-transform: lowercase;}
p.raw {text-transform: none;}

<h1>The heading-one at the beginninG</h1>
<p> By default, text is displayed in the capitalization it has in the source
document, but <strong>it is possible to change this</strong> using
the property 'text-transform'.
</p>
<p class="cummings">
For example, one could Create TEXT such as might have been Written by
the late Poet e.e.cummings.
</p>
<p class="raw">
If you feel the need to Explicitly Declare the transformation of text
to be 'none', that can be done as well.
</p>
```

## The Heading-one At The BeginninG

By default, text is displayed in the capitalization it has in the source document, but **IT IS POSSIBLE TO CHANGE THIS** using the property 'text-transform'.

for example, one could create text such as might have been written by the late poet e.e.cummings.

If you feel the need to Explicitly Declare the transformation of text to be 'none', that can be done as well.

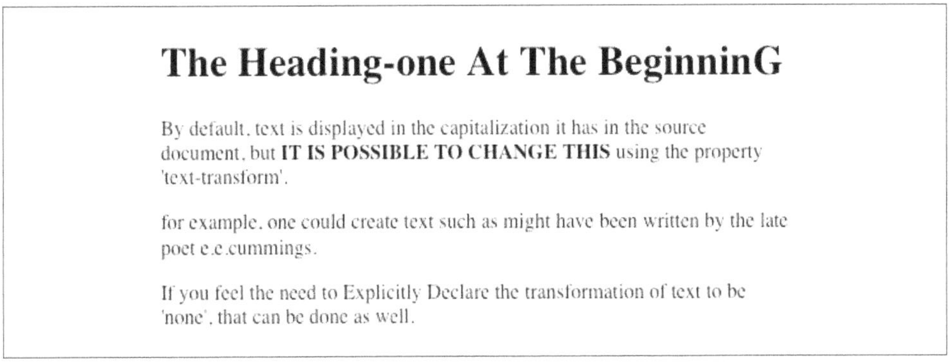

*Figure 28. Various kinds of text transformation*

Different user agents may have different ways of deciding where words begin and, as a result, which letters are capitalized. For example, the text "heading-one" in the h1 element, shown in Figure 28, could be rendered in one of two ways: "Heading-one" or "Heading-One." CSS does not say which is correct, so either is possible.

You probably also noticed that the last letter in the h1 element in Figure 28 is still uppercase. This is correct: when applying a text-transform of capitalize, CSS only requires user agents to make sure the first letter of each word is capitalized. They can ignore the rest of the word.

As a property, `text-transform` may seem minor, but it's very useful if you suddenly decide to capitalize all your h1 elements. Instead of individually changing the content of all your h1 elements, you can just use `text-transform` to make the change for you:

```
h1 {text-transform: uppercase;}

<h1>This is an H1 element</h1>
```

The advantages of using `text-transform` are twofold. First, you only need to write a single rule to make this change, rather than changing the h1 itself. Second, if you decide later to switch from all capitals back to initial capitals, the change is even easier, as Figure 29 shows:

```
h1 {text-transform: capitalize;}

<h1>This is an H1 element</h1>
```

---

## This Is An H1 Element

---

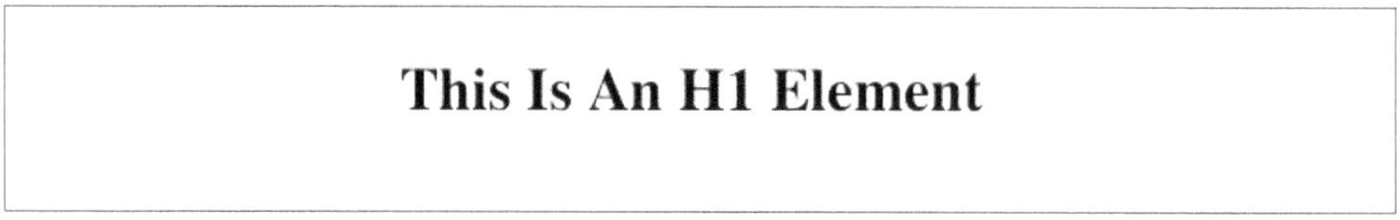

*Figure 29. Transforming an h1 element*

# Text Decoration

Next we come to `text-decoration`, which is a fascinating property that offers a whole truckload of interesting behaviors.

---

### text-decoration

*Values:*
    none | [ underline || overline || line-through || blink ] | inherit

*Initial value:*
    none

*Applies to:*
    All elements

*Inherited:*
    No

*Computed value:*
    As specified

---

As you might expect, underline causes an element to be underlined, just like the U element in HTML. overline causes the opposite effect—drawing a line across the top of the text. The value line-through draws a line straight through the middle of the text, which is also known as *strikethrough text* and is equivalent to the S and strike elements in HTML. blink causes the text to blink on and off, just like the much-maligned blink tag supported by Netscape. Figure 30 shows examples of each of these values:

```
p.emph {text-decoration: underline;}
p.topper {text-decoration: overline;}
p.old {text-decoration: line-through;}
p.annoy {text-decoration: blink;}
p.plain {text-decoration: none;}
```

The text of this paragraph, which has a class of 'one', is underlined.

The text of this paragraph, which has a class of 'two', is overlined.

The text of this paragraph, which has a class of 'three', is stricken (line-through).

The text of this paragraph, which has a class of 'four', is blinking (trust us).

The text of this paragraph, which has a class of 'five', has no decoration of any kind.

*Figure 30. Various kinds of text decoration*

 It's impossible to show the effect of blink in print, of course, but it's easy enough to imagine (perhaps all too easy). Incidentally, user agents are not required to actually blink blink text, and as of this writing, all known user agents were dropping or had dropped support for the blinking effect. (Internet Explorer never had it.)

The value none turns off any decoration that might otherwise have been applied to an element. Usually, undecorated text is the default appearance, but not always. For example, links are usually underlined by default. If you want to suppress the underlining of hyperlinks, you can use the following CSS rule to do so:

```
a {text-decoration: none;}
```

If you explicitly turn off link underlining with this sort of rule, the only visual difference between the anchors and normal text will be their color (at least by default, though there's no ironclad guarantee that there will be a difference in their colors).

Although I personally don't have a problem with it, many users are annoyed when they realize you've turned off link underlining. It's a matter of opinion, so let your own tastes be your guide, but remember: if your link colors aren't sufficiently different from normal text, users may have a hard time finding hyperlinks in your documents, particularly users with one form or another of color blindness.

You can also combine decorations in a single rule. If you want all hyperlinks to be both underlined and overlined, the rule is:

```
a:link, a:visited {text-decoration: underline overline;}
```

Be careful, though: if you have two different decorations matched to the same element, the value of the rule that wins out will completely replace the value of the loser. Consider:

```
h2.stricken {text-decoration: line-through;}
h2 {text-decoration: underline overline;}
```

Given these rules, any h2 element with a class of stricken will have only a line-through decoration. The underline and overline decorations are lost, since shorthand values replace one another instead of accumulating.

## Weird Decorations

Now, let's look into the unusual side of text-decoration. The first oddity is that text-decoration is *not* inherited. No inheritance implies that any decoration lines drawn with the text—under, over, or through it—will be the same color as the parent element. This is true even if the descendant elements are a different color, as depicted in Figure 31:

```
p {text-decoration: underline; color: black;}
strong {color: gray;}

<p>This paragraph, which is black and has a black underline, also contains
<strong>strongly emphasized text</strong> which has the black underline
beneath it as well.</p>
```

This paragraph, which is black and has a black underline, also contains strongly emphasized text which has the black underline beneath it as well.

*Figure 31. Color consistency in underlines*

Why is this so? Because the value of text-decoration is not inherited, the strong element assumes a default value of none. Therefore, the strong element has *no* underline. Now, there is very clearly a line under the strong element, so it seems silly to say that it has none. Nevertheless, it doesn't. What you see under the strong element is the paragraph's underline, which is effectively "spanning" the strong element. You can see it more clearly if you alter the styles for the boldface element, like this:

```
p {text-decoration: underline; color: black;}
strong {color: gray; text-decoration: none;}

<p>This paragraph, which is black and has a black underline, also contains
<strong>strongly emphasized text</strong> which has the black underline beneath
it as well.</p>
```

The result is identical to the one shown in Figure 31, since all you've done is to explicitly declare what was already the case. In other words, there is no way to turn off underlining (or overlining or a line-through) generated by a parent element.

When text-decoration is combined with vertical-align, even stranger things can happen. Figure 32 shows one of these oddities. Since the sup element has no decoration of its own, but it is elevated within an overlined element, the overline cuts through the middle of the sup element:

```
p {text-decoration: overline; font-size: 12pt;}
sup {vertical-align: 50%; font-size: 12pt;}
```

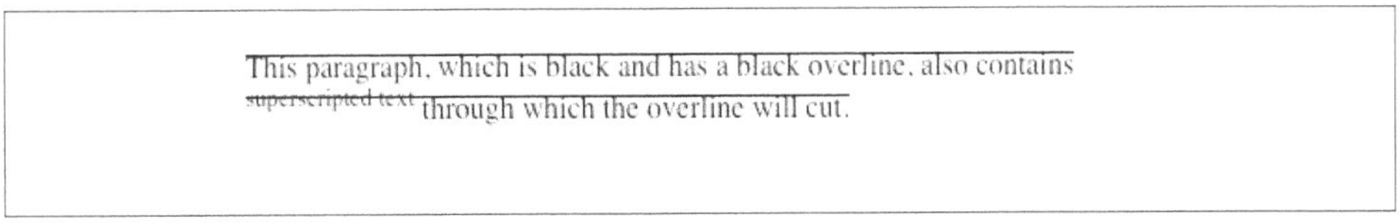

This paragraph, which is black and has a black overline, also contains superscripted text through which the overline will cut.

*Figure 32. Correct, although strange, decorative behavior*

By now you may be vowing never to use text decorations because of all the problems they could create. In fact, I've given you the simplest possible outcomes since we've explored only the way things *should* work according to the specification. In reality, some web browsers do turn off underlining in child elements, even though they aren't supposed to. The reason browsers violate the specification is simple enough: author expectations. Consider this markup:

```
p {text-decoration: underline; color: black;}
strong {color: silver; text-decoration: none;}

<p>This paragraph, which is black and has a black underline, also contains
<strong>boldfaced text</strong> which does not have black underline
beneath it.</p>
```

Figure 33 shows the display in a web browser that has switched off the underlining for the strong element.

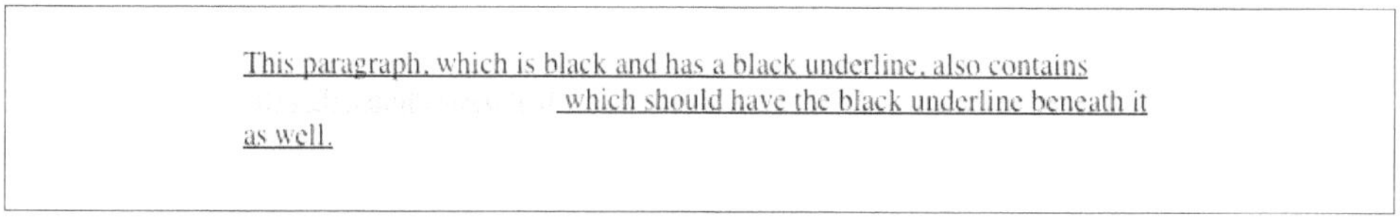

This paragraph, which is black and has a black underline, also contains
which should have the black underline beneath it
as well.

*Figure 33. How some browsers really behave*

The caveat here is that many browsers *do* follow the specification, and future versions of existing browsers (or any other user agents) might one day follow the specification precisely. If you depend on using none to suppress decorations, it's important to realize that it may come back to haunt you in the future, or even cause you problems in the present. Then again, future versions of CSS may include the means to turn off decorations without using none incorrectly, so maybe there's hope.

There is a way to change the color of a decoration without violating the specification. As you'll recall, setting a text decoration on an element means that the entire element has the same color decoration, even if there are child elements of different colors. To match the decoration color with an element, you must explicitly declare its decoration, as follows:

```
p {text-decoration: underline; color: black;}
strong {color: silver; text-decoration: underline;}

<p>This paragraph, which is black and has a black underline, also contains
<strong>strongly emphasized text</strong> which has the black underline
beneath it as well, but whose gray underline overlays the black underline
of its parent.</p>
```

In Figure 34, the strong element is set to be gray and to have an underline. The gray underline visually "overwrites" the parent's black underline, so the decoration's color matches the color of the strong element.

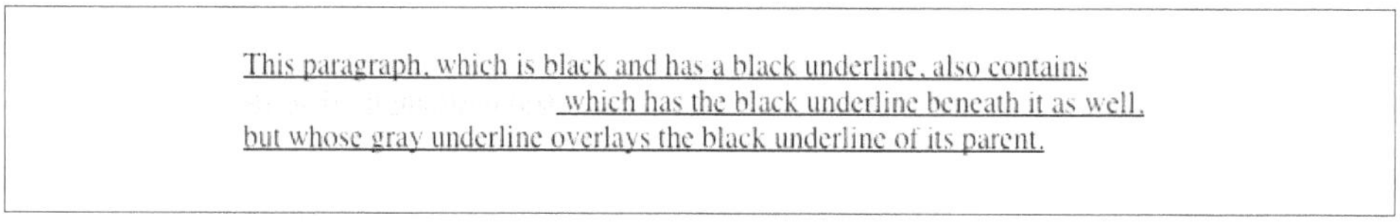

This paragraph, which is black and has a black underline, also contains
which has the black underline beneath it as well,
but whose gray underline overlays the black underline of its parent.

*Figure 34. Overcoming the default behavior of underlines*

# Text Rendering

A recent addition to CSS is `text-rendering`, which is actually an SVG property that is nevertheless treated as CSS by supporting user agents. It lets authors indicate what the user agent should prioritize when displaying text.

---

### text-rendering

*Values:*
    auto | optimizeSpeed | optimizeLegibility | geometricPrecision | inherit

*Initial value:*
    auto

*Applies to:*
    All elements

*Inherited:*
    Yes

---

The values `optimizeSpeed` and `optimizeLegibility` are relatively self-explanatory, indicating that drawing speed should be favored over legibility features like kerning and ligatures (for `optimizeSpeed`) or vice versa (for `optimizeLegibility`).

The precise legibility features that are used with `optimizeLegibility` are not explicitly defined, and the text rendering often depends on the operating system on which the user agent is running, so the exact results may vary. Figure 35 shows the results of `optimizeLegibility` in various browsers.

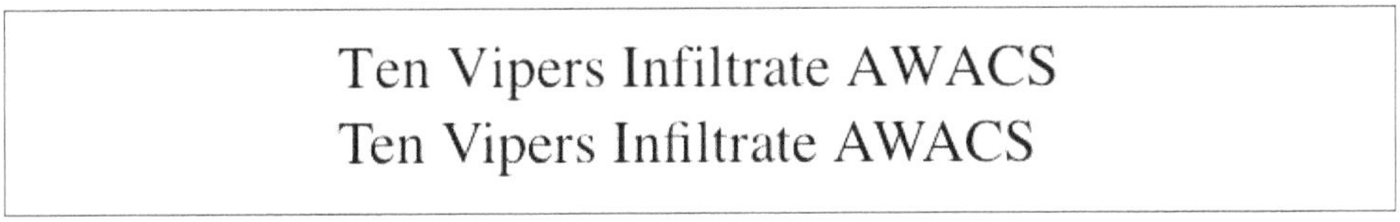

Ten Vipers Infiltrate AWACS
Ten Vipers Infiltrate AWACS

*Figure 35. Optimized legibility*

As you can see in Figure 35, the differences between optimized and non-optimized text are objectively rather small, but they can have a noticeable impact on readability.

The value `geometricPrecision`, on the other hand, directs the user agent to draw the text as precisely as possible, such that it could be scaled up or down with no loss of fidelity. You might think that this is always the case, but not so. Some fonts change kerning or ligature effects at different text sizes, for example, providing more kerning space at smaller sizes and tightening up the kerning space as the size is increased. With `geometricPrecision`, those hints are ignored. If it helps, think of it as the user agent drawing the text as though all the text is a series of SVG paths, not font glyphs.

Even by the usual standards of standards, the value `auto` is pretty vaguely defined in SVG:

> ...the user agent shall make appropriate tradeoffs to balance speed, legibility and geometric precision, but with legibility given more importance than speed and geometric precision.

That's it: user agents get to do what they think is appropriate, leaning towards legibility. In practice, things are more complicated. As an example, WebKit (as of mid-2013) seems to treat `optimizeLegibility` and `geometricPecision` as the same, while `auto` is equivalent to `optimizeSpeed`. In the former case, WebKit enables a series of font features in order to increase the legibility; these are disabled for `optimizeSpeed` and `auto`. Gecko, on the other hand, is reported to treat `auto` as `optimizeSpeed` for text sizes at or below 20px, and as `optimizeLegibility` for sizes above 20px.

# Text Shadows

CSS2 introduced a property for adding drop shadows to text. It was dropped from CSS 2.1 due to lack of implementation, but the web has moved on and `text-shadow` is now very widely supported.

---

### text-shadow

*Values:*
    none | [<*color*> || <*length*> <*length*> <*length*>? ,]* [<*color*> || <*length*>
    <*length*> <*length*>?] | inherit

*Initial value:*
    none

*Applies to:*
    All elements

*Inherited:*
    No

---

The obvious default is to not have a drop shadow for text. Otherwise, it's possible to define one or more shadows. Each shadow is defined by an optional color and three length values, the last of which is also optional.

The color sets the shadow's color, of course, so it's possible to define green, purple, or even white shadows. If the color is omitted, the shadow will be the same color as the text.

The first two length values determine the offset distance of the shadow from the text; the first is the horizontal offset and the second is the vertical offset. To define a solid, un-blurred green shadow offset five pixels to the right and half an em down from the text, as shown in Figure 36, you would write:

```
text-shadow: green 5px 0.5em;
```

Negative lengths cause the shadow to be offset to the left and upward from the original text. The following, also shown in Figure 36, places a light blue shadow five pixels to the left and half an em above the text:

```
text-shadow: rgb(128,128,255) -5px -0.5em;
```

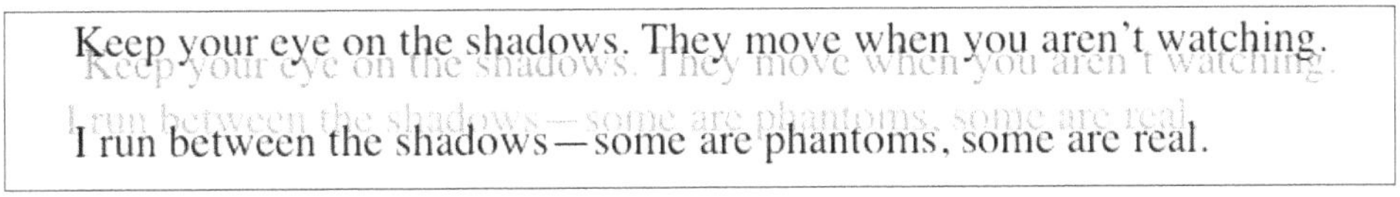

Keep your eye on the shadows. They move when you aren't watching.

I run between the shadows—some are phantoms, some are real.

*Figure 36. Simple shadows*

The optional third length value defines a "blur radius" for the shadow. The blur radius is defined as the distance from the shadow's outline to the edge of the blurring effect. A radius of two pixels would result in blurring that fills the space between the shadow's outline and the edge of the blurring. The exact blurring method is not defined, so different user agents might employ different effects. As an example, the following styles are rendered as shown in Figure 37:

```
p.cl1 {color: black; text-shadow: gray 2px 2px 4px;}
p.cl2 {color: white; text-shadow: 0 0 4px black;}
p.cl3 {color: black; text-shadow: 1em 0.5em 5px red, -0.5em -1em hsla(100,75%,
25%,0.33);}
```

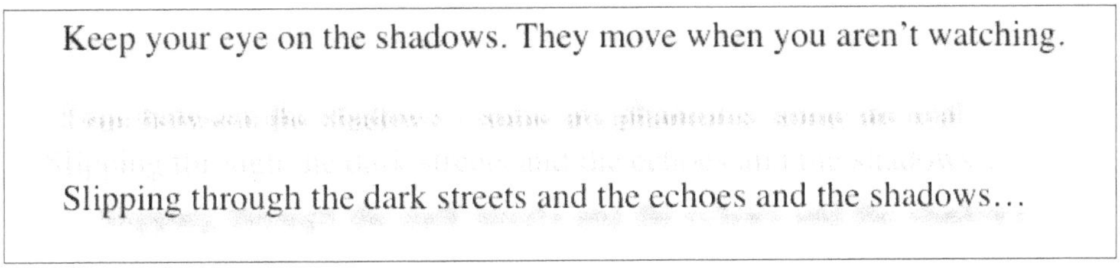

Keep your eye on the shadows. They move when you aren't watching.

Slipping through the dark streets and the echoes and the shadows…

*Figure 37. Dropping shadows all over*

Note that large numbers of text shadows, or text shadows with very large blur values, can create performance slowdowns, particularly in low-power and CPU-constrained situations such as mobile devices. Authors are advised to test thoroughly before deploying public designs that use text shadows.

# Handling White Space

Now that we've covered a variety of ways to style the text, let's talk about the property white-space, which affects the user agent's handling of space, newline, and tab characters within the document source.

---

## white-space

*Values:*
    normal | nowrap | pre | pre-wrap | pre-line | inherit

*Initial value:*
    normal

*Applies to:*
    All elements (CSS 2.1); block-level elements (CSS1 and CSS2)

*Inherited:*
    No

*Computed value:*
    As specified

---

Using this property, you can affect how a browser treats the white space between words and lines of text. To a certain extent, default XHTML handling already does this: it collapses any white space down to a single space. So given the following markup, the rendering in a web browser would show only one space between each word and ignore the linefeed in the elements:

```
<p>This     paragraph   has     many
    spaces          in it.</p>
```

You can explicitly set this default behavior with the following declaration:

```
p {white-space: normal;}
```

This rule tells the browser to do as browsers have always done: discard extra white space. Given this value, linefeed characters (carriage returns) are converted into spaces, and any sequence of more than one space in a row is converted to a single space.

Should you set white-space to pre, however, the white space in an affected element is treated as though the elements were XHTML pre elements; white space is *not* ignored, as shown in Figure 38:

```
p {white-space: pre;}

<p>This     paragraph   has      many
     spaces         in it.</p>
```

```
                         This   paragraph has    many
                            spaces    in it.
```

*Figure 38. Honoring the spaces in markup*

With a white-space value of pre, the browser will pay attention to extra spaces and even carriage returns. In this respect, and in this respect alone, any element can be made to act like a pre element.

The opposite value is nowrap, which prevents text from wrapping within an element, except wherever you use a br element. Using nowrap in CSS is much like setting a table cell not to wrap in HTML 4 with <td nowrap>, except the white-space value can be applied to any element. The effects of the following markup are shown in Figure 39:

```
<p style="white-space: nowrap;">This paragraph is not allowed to wrap,
which means that the only way to end a line is to insert a line-break
element.  If no such element is inserted, then the line will go forever,
forcing the user to scroll horizontally to read whatever can't be
initially displayed <br/>in the browser window.</p>
```

```
   This paragraph is not allowed to wrap, which means that the only way to end a line is to insert a line-bre
   in the browser window.
```

*Figure 39. Suppressing line wrapping with the white-space property*

You can actually use white-space to replace the nowrap attribute on table cells:

```
td {white-space: nowrap;}

<table><tr>
<td>The contents of this cell are not wrapped.</td>
<td>Neither are the contents of this cell.</td>
<td>Nor this one, or any after it, or any other cell in this table.</td>
<td>CSS prevents any wrapping from happening.</td>
</tr></table>
```

CSS 2.1 introduced the values pre-wrap and pre-line, which were absent in earlier versions of CSS. The effect of these values is to allow authors to better control white space handling.

If an element is set to pre-wrap, then text within that element has white space sequences preserved, but text lines are wrapped normally. With this value, line-breaks in the source and those that are generated are also honored. pre-line is the opposite of pre-wrap and causes white space sequences to collapse as in normal text but honors new lines. For example, consider the following markup, which is illustrated in Figure 40:

```
<p style="white-space: pre-wrap;">
This  paragraph      has  a  great    many    s p a c e s    within  its textual
    content,  but their    preservation      will    not    prevent    line
      wrapping or line breaking.
</p>
<p style="white-space: pre-line;">
This  paragraph      has  a  great    many    s p a c e s    within  its textual
    content,  but their collapse  will    not    prevent    line
      wrapping or line breaking.
</p>
```

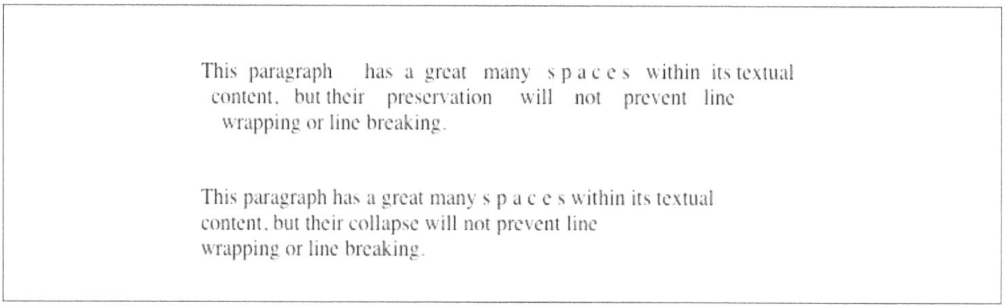

*Figure 40. Two different ways to handle white space*

Table 1 summarizes the behaviors of white-space properties.

*Table 1. White-space properties*

| Value | White space | Linefeeds | Auto line wrapping |
|---|---|---|---|
| pre-line | Collapsed | Honored | Allowed |
| normal | Collapsed | Ignored | Allowed |
| nowrap | Collapsed | Ignored | Prevented |
| pre | Preserved | Honored | Prevented |
| pre-wrap | Preserved | Honored | Allowed |

# Setting Tab Sizes

Since white space is preserved in some values of `white-space`, it stands to reason that tabs (i.e., Unicode code point 0009) will be displayed as, well, tabs. But how many spaces should each tab equal? That's where `tab-size` comes in.

---

## tab-size

*Values:*
    `<integer>` | `<length>` | `inherit`

*Initial value:*
    8

*Applies to:*
    Block elements

*Inherited:*
    Yes

*Computed value:*
    The absolute-length equivalent of the specified value

---

By default, any tab character will be treated the same as eight spaces in a row, but you can alter that by using a different integer value. Thus, `tab-size: 4` will cause each tab to be rendered the same as if it were four spaces in a row.

If a length value is supplied, then each tab is rendered using that length. For example, `tab-size: 10px` will cause a sequence of three tabs to be rendered as 30 pixels of white space. The effects of the following rules is illustrated in Figure 41.

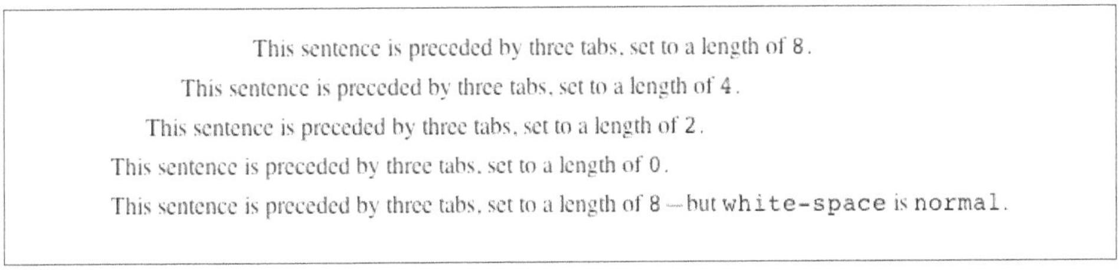

This sentence is preceded by three tabs, set to a length of 8.

This sentence is preceded by three tabs, set to a length of 4.

This sentence is preceded by three tabs, set to a length of 2.

This sentence is preceded by three tabs, set to a length of 0.

This sentence is preceded by three tabs, set to a length of 8 —but `white-space` is `normal`.

*Figure 41. Differing tab lengths*

Note that `tab-size` is effectively ignored when the value of `white-space` causes white space to be collapsed (see Table 1). The value will still be computed in such cases, of course, but there will be no visible effect no matter how many tabs appear in the source.

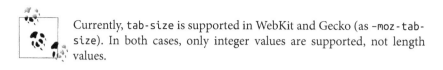

Currently, tab-size is supported in WebKit and Gecko (as -moz-tab-size). In both cases, only integer values are supported, not length values.

# Wrapping and Hyphenation

Hyphens can be very useful in situations where there are long words and short line lengths, such as blog posts on mobile devices and portions of *The Economist*. Authors can always insert their own hyphenation hints using the Unicode character U+00AD SOFT HYPHEN (or, in HTML, &shy;), but CSS also offers a way to enable hyphenation without littering up the document with hints.

---

## hyphens

*Values:*
    manual | auto | none | inherit

*Initial value:*
    manual

*Applies to:*
    All elements

*Inherited:*
    Yes

*Computed value:*
    As specified

---

With the default value of manual, hyphens are only inserted where there are manually-inserted hyphenation markers in the document, such as U+00AD or &shy;. Otherwise, no hyphenation occurs. The value none, on the other hand, suppresses any hyphenation, even if manual break markers are present; thus, U+00AD and &shy; are ignored.

The far more interesting (and potentially inconsistent) value is auto, which permits the browser to insert hyphens and break words at "appropriate" places inside words, even where no manually inserted hyphenation breaks exist. This leads to interesting questions like what constitutes a "word" and under what circumstances it is appropriate to hyphenate a word, both of which are highly language-dependent. User agents are supposed to prefer manually inserted hyphen breaks to automatically determined breaks, but there are no guarantees. An illustration of hyphenation, or the suppression thereof, in the following example is shown in Figure 42:

---

```
.cl01 {hyphens: auto;}
.cl02 {hyphens: manual;}
.cl03 {hyphens: none;}

<p    class="cl01">Supercalifragilisticexpialidocious    antidisestablishmentarian-
ism.</p>
<p    class="cl02">Supercalifragilisticexpialidocious    antidisestablishmentarian-
ism.</p>
<p class="cl02">Super&shy;cali&shy;fragi&shy;listic&shy;expi&shy;ali&shy;docious
anti&shy;dis&shy;establish&shy;ment&shy;arian&shy;ism.</p>
<p class="cl03">Super&shy;cali&shy;fragi&shy;listic&shy;expi&shy;ali&shy;docious
anti&shy;dis&shy;establish&shy;ment&shy;arian&shy;ism.</p>
```

| Supercalifragilisticexpialido-<br>cious antidisestablishmentar-<br>ianism. | Supercalifragilisticexpi-<br>alidocious antidisestab-<br>lishmentarianism. | Supercalifragilistic-<br>expialidocious an-<br>tidisestablishmen-<br>tarianism. |
| Supercalifragilisticexpialidocious<br>antidisestablishmentarianism. | Supercalifragilisticexpialidocious<br>antidisestablishmentarianism. | Supercalifragilisticexpialidocious<br>antidisestablishmentarianism. |
| Supercalifragilisticexpiali-<br>docious antidisestablishment-<br>arianism. | Supercalifragilisticexpi-<br>alidocious antidis-<br>establishmentarianism. | Supercalifragilistic-<br>expialidocious anti-<br>disestablishment-<br>arianism. |
| Supercalifragilisticexpialidocious<br>antidisestablishmentarianism. | Supercalifragilisticexpialidocious<br>antidisestablishmentarianism. | Supercalifragilisticexpialidocious<br>antidisestablishmentarianism. |

*Figure 42. Hyphenation results*

Because hyphenation is so language-dependent, and because the CSS specification does not define precise (or even vague) rules regarding how user agents should carry out hyphenation, there is every chance that hyphenation will be different from one browser to the next.

Furthermore, if you do choose to hyphenate, be careful about the elements to which you apply the hyphenation. hyphens is an inherited property, so simply declaring body {hyphens: auto;} will apply hyphenation to everything in your document—including textareas, code samples, blockquotes, and so on. Blocking automatic hyphenation at the level of those elements is probably a good idea, using rules something like this:

```
body {hyphens: auto;}
code, var, kbd, samp, tt, dir, listing, plaintext, xmp,
    abbr, acronym, blockquote, q, textarea, input, option {hyphens: manual;}
```

It's probably obvious why suppressing hyphenation in code samples and code blocks is desirable, especially in languages that use hyphens in things like property and value names. (Ahem.) Similar logic holds for keyboard input text—you definitely don't want a stray dash getting into your Unix command line examples! And so on down the line.

Of course, if you decide that you want to hyphenate some of these elements, just remove them from the selector. (It can be kind of fun to watch the text you're typing into a textarea get auto-hyphenated as you type it.)

 As of mid-2013, hyphens was supported by all major desktop browsers, albeit using vendor prefixes, as well as on many mobile browsers. As noted, such support is always language-dependent.

Hyphens can be suppressed by the effects of other properties, such as word-break, which affects how soft wrapping of text is calculated in various languages.

---

# word-break

*Values:*
    normal | break-all | keep-all | inherit

*Initial value:*
    normal

*Applies to:*
    All elements

*Inherited:*
    Yes

*Computed value:*
    As specified

---

When a run of text is too long to fit into a single line, it is "soft wrapped." This is in contrast to "hard wraps," which are things like linefeed characters and <br> elements. Where the text is soft-wrapped is determined by the user agent (or the OS it uses), but word-break lets authors influence its decision-making.

The default value of normal means that text should be wrapped like it always has been. In practical terms, this means that text is broken between words, though the definition of a word varies by language. In Latin-derived languages like English, this is almost always a space between letter sequences (e.g., words). In ideographic languages like Japanese, each symbol is a word, so breaks can occur between any two symbols. In other CJK languages, though, the soft-wrap points may be limited to appear between sequences of symbols that are not space-separated.

Again, that's all by default, and is the way browsers have handled text for years. If you apply the value break-all, then soft wrapping can (and will) occur between any two characters, even if they are in the middle of a word. With this value, no hyphens are shown, even if the soft wrapping occurs at a hyphenation point (see hyphens, earlier). Note that values of the line-break property (described next) can affect the behavior of break-all in CJK text.

keep-all, on the other hand, suppresses soft wrapping between characters, even in CJK languages where each symbol is a word. Thus, in Japanese, a sequence of symbols with no white space will not be soft wrapped, even if this means the text line will exceed the length of its element. (This behavior is similar to white-space: pre.)

Figure 43 shows a few examples of word-break values, and Table 2 summarizes the effects of each value.

*Figure 43. Altering word breaking behavior*

*Table 2. Word-breaking behavior*

| Value | Non-CJK | CJK | Hyphenation permitted |
|---|---|---|---|
| normal | As usual | As usual | Yes |
| break-all | After any character | After any character | No |
| keep-all | As usual | Around sequences | Yes |

If your interests run to CJK text, then in addition to word-break you will also want to get to know line-break.

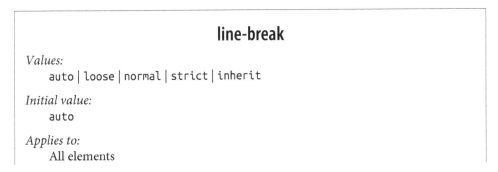

# line-break

*Values:*
    auto | loose | normal | strict | inherit

*Initial value:*
    auto

*Applies to:*
    All elements

*Inherited:*
    Yes

*Computed value:*
    As specified

As we just saw, `word-break` can affect how lines of text are soft-wrapped in CJK text. The `line-break` property also affects such soft wrapping: specifically how wrapping is handled around CJK-specific symbols as well as around non-CJK punctuation (such as exclamation points, hyphens, and ellipses) that appears in text declared to be CJK.

In other words, `line-break` applies to certain CJK characters all the time, regardless of the content's declared language. If you throw some CJK characters into a paragraph of English text, `line-break` will still apply to them, but not to anything else in the text. Conversely, if you declare content to be in a CJK language, `line-break` will continue to apply to those CJK characters *plus* a number of non-CJK characters within the CJK text. These include punctuation marks, currency symbols, and a few other symbols.

There is no authoritative list of which characters are affected and which are not, but the specification (*http://w3.org/TR/css3-text/#line-break*) provides a list of recommended symbols and behaviors around those symbols.

The default value `auto` allows user agents to soft wrap text as they like, and more importantly lets UAs vary the line-breaking they do based on the situation. Thus, for example, the UA can use looser line-breaking rules for short lines of text and stricter rules for long lines. In effect, `auto` allows the user agent to switch between the `loose`, `normal`, and `strict` values as needed, possibly even on a line-by-line basis within a single element.

Doubtless you can infer that those other values have the following general meanings:

`loose`
    This value imposes the "least restrictive" rules for wrapping text, and is meant for use when line lengths are short, such as in newspapers.

`normal`
    This value imposes the "most common" rules for wrapping text. What exactly "most common" means is not precisely defined, though there is the aforementioned list of recommended behaviors.

`strict`
    This value imposes the "most stringent" rules for wrapping text. Again, this is not precisely defined.

# Wrapping Text

After all that information about hyphenation and soft wrapping, what happens when text overflows its container anyway? That's what overflow-wrap addresses.

---

## overflow-wrap (neé word-wrap)

*Values:*
    normal | break-word | inherit

*Initial value:*
    -

*Applies to:*
    All elements

*Inherited:*
    Yes

*Computed value:*
    -

---

For once, this property couldn't be more straightforward. If the default value of normal is in effect, then wrapping happens as normal (obviously!); which is to say, between words or as directed by the language. If break-word is in effect, then wrapping can happen in the middle of words. Figure 44 illustrates the difference.

Supercalifragilisticexpialidociously awesome antidisestablishmentarianism.    Supercalifragilisticexpialidoc iously awesome antidisestablishmentarianism.

*Figure 44. Overflow wrapping*

 Note that overflow-wrap can only operate if the value of white-space allows line wrapping. If it does not (e.g., with the value pre), then overflow-wrap has no effect.

Where overflow-wrap gets complicated is in its history and implementation. Once upon a time there was a property called word-wrap that did exactly what overflow-wrap does. The two are so identical that the specification specifically states that user agents "...must treat word-wrap as an alternate name for the overflow-wrap property, as if it were a shorthand of overflow-wrap."

Of course, browsers don't always do this. As of mid-2013, IE, Firefox, and Safari honored word-wrap but not overflow-wrap; Blackberry, Opera, and Chrome (and, presumably, Blink) honored both. For this reason, it's actually better to use word-wrap, despite it being the vaguely deprecated version. If you want to future-proof, use both:

```
pre {word-wrap: break-word; overflow-wrap: break-word;}
```

While overflow-wrap: break-word may appear very similar to word-break: break-all, they are not the same thing. To see why, compare the second box in Figure 44 to the top middle box in Figure 43. As you can see, overflow-wrap only kicks in if content actually overflows; thus, when there is an opportunity to use white space in the source to wrap lines, overflow-wrap will take it. By contrast, word-break: break-all will cause wrapping when content reaches the wrapping edge, regardless of any whitespace that comes earlier in the line.

# Text Direction

If you're reading this book in English or any number of other languages, then you're reading the text left to right and top to bottom, which is the flow direction of English. Not every language runs this way, of course. There are many right-to-left and top-to-bottom languages such as Hebrew and Arabic, and CSS2 introduced a property to describe their directionality.

---

## direction

*Values:*
    ltr | rtl | inherit

*Initial value:*
    ltr

*Applies to:*
    All elements

*Inherited:*
    Yes

*Computed value:*
    As specified

---

The direction property affects the writing direction of text in a block-level element, the direction of table column layout, the direction in which content horizontally overflows its element box, and the position of the last line of a fully justified element. For inline elements, direction applies only if the property `unicode-bidi` is set to either `embed` or `bidi-override`. (See below for a description of `unicode-bidi`.)

 Before CSS3, CSS included no provisions in the specification for top-to-bottom languages. As of this writing, the CSS3 Text Module is a Candidate Recommendation, and it addresses this point with a new property called `writing-mode`, which was poorly supported as of mid-2013.

Although `ltr` is the default, it is expected that if a browser is displaying right-to-left text, the value will be changed to `rtl`. Thus, a browser might carry an internal rule stating something like the following:

```
*:lang(ar), *:lang(he) {direction: rtl;}
```

The real rule would be longer and encompass all right-to-left languages, not just Arabic and Hebrew, but it illustrates the point.

While CSS attempts to address writing direction, Unicode has a much more robust method for handling directionality. With the property `unicode-bidi`, CSS authors can take advantage of some of Unicode's capabilities.

---

# unicode-bidi

*Values:*
    `normal` | `embed` | `bidi-override` | `inherit`

*Initial value:*
    `normal`

*Applies to:*
    All elements

*Inherited:*
    No

*Computed value:*
    As specified

---

Here we'll simply quote the value descriptions from the CSS 2.1 specification, which do a good job of capturing the essence of each value:

normal

> The element does not open an additional level of embedding with respect to the bidirectional algorithm. For inline-level elements, implicit reordering works across element boundaries.

embed

> If the element is inline-level, this value opens an additional level of embedding with respect to the bidirectional algorithm. The direction of this embedding level is given by the `direction` property. Inside the element, reordering is done implicitly. This corresponds to adding an LRE (U+202A; for `direction: ltr`) or an RLE (U+202B; for `direction: rtl`) at the start of the element and a PDF (U+202C) at the end of the element.

bidi-override

> This creates an override for inline-level elements. For block-level elements, this creates an override for inline-level descendants not within another block. This means that, inside the element, reordering is strictly in sequence according to the `direction` property; the implicit part of the bidirectional algorithm is ignored. This corresponds to adding an LRO (U+202D; for `direction: ltr`) or RLO (U+202E; for `direction: rtl`) at the start of the element and a PDF (U+202C) at the end of the element.

# Summary

Even without altering the font face, there are many ways to change the appearance of text. There are classic effects such as underlining, of course, but CSS also enables you to draw lines over text or through it, change the amount of space between words and letters, indent the first line of a paragraph (or other block-level element), align text in various ways, exert influence over the hyphenation and line-breaking of text, and much more. You can even alter the amount of space between lines of text. There is also support in CSS for languages other than those that are written left-to-right, top-to-bottom. Given that so much of the Web is text, the strength of these properties makes a great deal of sense. Recent developments in improving text legibility and placement are likely only the beginnings of what we will eventually be able to do with regards to text styling.

## About the Author

**Eric A. Meyer** has been working with the Web since late 1993 and is an internationally recognized expert on the subjects of HTML, CSS, and web standards. A widely read author, he is a past member of the CSS&FP Working Group and was the primary creator of the W3C's CSS1 Test Suite. In 2006, Eric was inducted into the International Academy of Digital Arts and Sciences for "international recognition on the topics of HTML and CSS" and helping to "inform excellence and efficiency on the Web."

Eric is currently the principal founder at Complex Spiral Consulting, which counts among its clients a wide variety of corporations, educational institutions, and government agencies. He is also, along with Jeffrey Zeldman, co-founder of An Event Apart ("The design conference for people who make websites"), and he speaks regularly at that conference as well as many others. Eric lives with his family in Cleveland, Ohio, which is a much nicer city than you've been led to believe. A historian by training and inclination, he enjoys a good meal whenever he can and considers almost every form of music to be worthwhile.

## Colophon

The animal on the cover of *CSS Text* is a salmon (*Salmonidae* family).

The cover image is from Dover Pictorial Archive. The cover font is Adobe ITC Garamond. The text font is Adobe Minion Pro; the heading font is Adobe Myriad Condensed; and the code font is Dalton Maag's Ubuntu Mono.

# Have it your way.

# Get even more for your money.

**Join the O'Reilly Community, and register the O'Reilly books you own. It's free, and you'll get:**

- $4.99 ebook upgrade offer
- 40% upgrade offer on O'Reilly print books
- Membership discounts on books and events
- Free lifetime updates to ebooks and videos
- Multiple ebook formats, DRM FREE
- Participation in the O'Reilly community
- Newsletters
- Account management
- 100% Satisfaction Guarantee

**Signing up is easy:**

1. **Go to: oreilly.com/go/register**
2. **Create an O'Reilly login.**
3. **Provide your address.**
4. **Register your books.**

Note: English-language books only

**To order books online:**
oreilly.com/store

**For questions about products or an order:**
orders@oreilly.com

**To sign up to get topic-specific email announcements and/or news about upcoming books, conferences, special offers, and new technologies:**
elists@oreilly.com

**For technical questions about book content:**
booktech@oreilly.com

**To submit new book proposals to our editors:**
proposals@oreilly.com

**O'Reilly books are available in multiple DRM-free ebook formats. For more information:**
oreilly.com/ebooks

O'REILLY®

Spreading the knowledge of innovators                    oreilly.com

9 781449 373740